W9-DCL-152

EDGE
BOOKS™

WILD MOMENTs OF
SPORTS CAR RACING

BY M. WEBER

CAPSTONE PRESS
a capstone imprint

Edge Books are published by Capstone Press,
1710 Roe Crest Drive, North Mankato, Minnesota 56003
www.mycapstone.com

Library of Congress Cataloging-in-Publication Data
Library of Congress Cataloging-in-Publication data is available on the Library of Congress Website
ISBN 978-1-5157-7405-1 (library binding)
ISBN 978-1-5157-7409-9 (eBook PDF)

Editorial Credits
Lauren Dupuis-Perez, editor; Sara Radka, designer; Laura Manthe, production specialist

Quote Sources
p.9, "OultonPark2008 Hunter Abbott Big Crash." YouTube, https://youtu.be/2nCnZSGn4a4, November 16,
2016; p.15, "2013 Grand Prix of Baltimore." Guy Cosmo, http://www.guycosmo.com/2013-grand-prix-of-
baltimore; p.27, "Brendon Hartley in spectacular crash at World Endurance Championship race at Silverstone."
Stuff. N.p., April 19, 2016

Photo Credits
Newscom: ZUMAPRESS/James Moy, cover; Shutterstock: Chatchai Somwat, 5; Shutterstock: Joseph Sohm, 7;
Shutterstock: Christoff, 9; Newscom: Lloyd Fox/Baltimore Sun/MCT, 11; Newscom: ZUMAPRESS/Panoramic,
12, 18; Shutterstock: Action Sports Photography, 13; Newscom: ZUMAPRESS/Ron Bijlsma, 14; Getty Images:
Brian Cleary, 15; Getty Images: Ker Robertson, 16, 26 (bottom); Shutterstock: Oskar Schuler, 17 (top), 27;
Newscom: ZUMAPRESS/Dpi/NurPhoto, 17 (bottom); Newscom: Mirrorpix, 19; Newscom: Del Mecum/
Cal Sport Media, 20; Newscom: Alexis Goure/SIPA, 23; Newscom: Getty Images/Dean Treml/Red Bull, 25;
Wikimedia: Wolkenkratzer, 28

Graphic elements by Book Buddy Media.

The publisher does not endorse products whose logos may appear on objects in images in this book.

Printed in the United States of America.
010364F17

TABLE OF CONTENTS

SPEED AND STYLE

Everyone loves to spot a sports car on the road. These fast and stylish cars are known for their speed and engineering. The famous car makers that build these cars also produce sports cars for professional racing. Some of these cars are similar to the sports cars you see on the road. But they're fine-tuned for racing. They can be split into two categories. **Grand touring** cars are more similar to road cars. **Prototypes** are specially made for racing. Sports car racetracks are twisting and varied, making each race unique. The races often run for long periods of time, and drivers often work in teams to win.

No matter the race or length of the track, every driver aims for speed. Race cars are built to be as fast as possible. Their high-powered engines and bodies are built to be **aerodynamic** on the road. These high-speed races can result in unforgettable action and some pretty wild moments.

grand touring—a type of sports car built for long-distance racing and based on models available for consumers

prototype—a type of sports car, which is based on a model available to consumers, used at the highest level of racing

aerodynamic—built to move easily through the air

It takes seven to 10 days to build the outside of a sports car, called a chassis.

CHAPTER 1

CRASHED TO EARTH

Sports car racing has been popular for many decades. The cars have changed over the years, but the excitement of the race has not. In 1982 Bill Maier entered a race in California. When testing the car before the race, his team was concerned about his brakes. But Maier's car was cleared to enter the race at a California track known as Laguna Seca. Little did he know, his brakes would be the least of his problems.

Maier began the race at the back of the pack, already at a disadvantage. He raced toward the front of the pack and caught up to his **competitors**. Maier entered Turn 1 in the middle of a cluster of cars. He had to pull to the far edge to find space to pass. Just then, a Porsche came up next to him and closed in on the open space. Maier couldn't move away from the cars around him. His Mustang was forced into the low hill next to the track. A spray of earth and dirt flew into the air as Maier flipped and rolled.

It took a few minutes for the dust to clear around the wrecked car. When it did, fans saw Maier emerge from his car unhurt, but out of the race.

competitor—a person who tries to win a race or contest

At the time of Bill Maier's 1982 race, Laguna Seca was 1.9 miles (3 kilometers) of racetrack. Just five years later, the track was lengthened to 2.2 miles (3.6 km).

WILD! The first recorded automobile race took place in 1884 over a 50-mile (80.5-km) distance. The average speed was just 10.2 miles (16.4 km) per hour.

CHAPTER 2

FIERY END

There are many dangers involved in the wild world of sports car racing. Drivers must be prepared to handle both big and small emergencies. A small issue, such as two cars bumping against each other, can quickly become a larger problem.

In 2008 Hunter Abbott entered the British GT Championship season-opener. It was held at Oulton Park in England. Abbott was driving a Ginetta G50. The race was set to take around an hour. About 10 minutes into the race, Abbott had to navigate an S-shaped turn. During the turn, Peter Snowdon tapped Abbott's car with his Aston Martin. The high-speed bump caused Abbott to veer off the track at 100 miles (161 km) per hour. He was headed straight for the track barriers.

Abbott's car broke through the barrier and barrel-rolled across the ground. When it stopped the car burst into flames. Fans watched in horror as he struggled to free himself. They cheered when he was successful. Rescue crews quickly arrived to put out the flames and get Abbott into an ambulance.

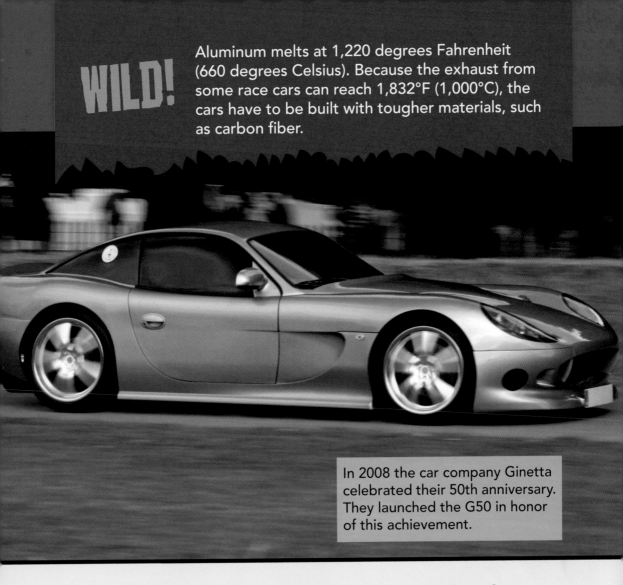

Aluminum melts at 1,220 degrees Fahrenheit (660 degrees Celsius). Because the exhaust from some race cars can reach 1,832°F (1,000°C), the cars have to be built with tougher materials, such as carbon fiber.

In 2008 the car company Ginetta celebrated their 50th anniversary. They launched the G50 in honor of this achievement.

The race was delayed, but soon continued. Abbott's car was destroyed, but he walked away with only minor burns and injuries. After the crash he said, "I can safely say that was the scariest moment of my life ... far and away the worst accident I've ever had in a motor race, and I'm just glad to be here."

When Abbott returned to racing two weeks later, he was able to come away with a victory.

CHAPTER 3

BREAKING BARRIERS

Every driver enters a race hoping to cross the finish line before everyone else. But sometimes there is no predicting where a driver might find himself at the end of a race. Two drivers saw that for themselves after they joined the American Le Mans Series. The race was held in 2013 at the Virginia International Raceway.

Eduardo Cisneros and Marco Holzer, both driving Porsche 911s, were fighting for the lead down a long, straight strip of the track. They were coming up on a turn when the two cars veered into each other. This sent the cars flying. They headed straight for the tire wall barrier. Both cars rolled. Cisneros' car flipped over multiple times. The last flip sent him high into the air. When his car crashed down, it came to rest on top of the barrier!

Eduardo Cisneros drives the #29 Porsche 911.

Marco Holzer, in the white Porsche, is a German sports car driver. He has raced in the American Le Mans Series as well as the 24 Hours of Le Mans.

Both Cisneros and Holzer were shaken, but glad to have survived the crash. When they pulled themselves from their wrecked cars they smiled and gave the crowd a thumbs-up.

LE MANS IN AMERICA

In 1999 the American Le Mans Series was created. It was modeled on the famous European race, 24 Hours of Le Mans. It began as a series of eight races and grew to a total of 12 races. These races followed the same rules as their European counterparts. They included rules on the length of races and the size of each racing team. In 2014 the American Le Mans Series merged with another racing series to become the United SportsCar Championship. The new series also brought new competition **classes** to decide which types of cars can race against each other. In 2016 this series was renamed the WeatherTech SportsCar Championships.

class—a group of things that are similar in many ways

CHAPTER 4

ROUGH START

One missed maneuver sent several cars spinning, bumping, and crashing into each other at the 2013 Baltimore Grand Prix.

The dangers of racing in a pack quickly became apparent at the start of the Baltimore **Grand Prix** in 2013. The race was just beginning, and sports cars were getting into place. This is an important time for drivers to get ahead. But one small mistake can stop the race before it begins.

Grand Prix—any of a series of auto racing or motorcycling contests forming part of a championship series, held in various locations

As the cars started to race, driver Scott Tucker was searching for the best position, with little space to move. Suddenly, Tucker's car was tapped from behind. The small bump sent both cars spinning. This quickly led to a series of spins and bumps. Three cars ended up sideways in a line across the track. There were almost a dozen cars still behind the pack that had to stop. The result was a lengthy delay as crews cleaned up wrecked cars from the course.

Simon Pagenaud

There were no serious injuries in the pileup, but it was just the beginning of a frustrating race. It was delayed twice more for false starts. A second three-car pileup happened later on. Tucker's racemate Guy Cosmo avoided the accidents. He said, "The race was just insane — lots of crashes, yellows and the long red flag from the crash at the start — suddenly we had an even shorter sprint race. When we finally got under way, it was time to get to the front as quick as possible."

In the end, it was driver Simon Pagenaud, who had also managed to stay out of the race's accidents, who won.

CHAPTER 5

UPSIDE-DOWN ENDING

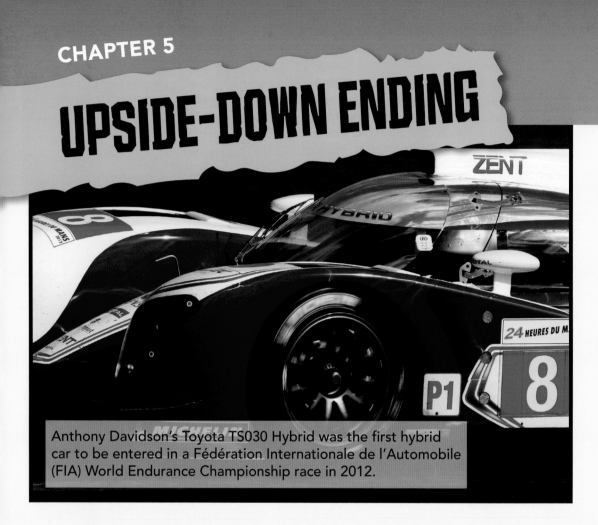

Anthony Davidson's Toyota TS030 Hybrid was the first hybrid car to be entered in a Fédération Internationale de l'Automobile (FIA) World Endurance Championship race in 2012.

On one of the shortest nights of the year, drivers get behind the wheels of their race cars to take part in one of racing's grandest competitions. The 24 Hours of Le Mans is a sports car **endurance** race that covers a course of 8.5 miles (13.7 km) near Le Mans, France. The winner is the racer who can cover the most ground in 24 hours. The race is designed to push drivers to their limits.

endurance—the ability to keep doing an activity for long periods of time

On June 17th, 2012, the race was more than just a test of stamina for Anthony Davidson and Piergiuseppe Perazzini. It would test their ability to recover when the unexpected happened.

Anthony Davidson

Davidson was speeding into a corner. He had just lost the lead in the race and was eager to gain it back. Davidson was roaring at 190 miles (306 km) per hour. Just at that moment, Perazzini came up from behind and tried to cut him off at the turn. The cars made contact, flipping Davidson's car into the air, with a back-over-front somersault. He finally came to a stop, skidding against the tire barrier. Perazzini also lost control. His car slammed into the tire barrier and flipped over. Perazzini's car came to rest on its roof, with the tires spinning in the air.

Piergiuseppe Perazzini

Piergiuseppe Perazzini was born in Florence, Italy. He drives a Ferrari 458 that is painted red, white, and green, which are the colors of the Italian flag.

The test was over for Davidson and Perazzini. They were out of the race. Davidson had to spend some time in the hospital to repair a broken back, and Perazzini walked away, disappointed. Both men remained determined to race again.

Graham Hill

KING WITH A "TRIPLE CROWN"

The "Triple Crown of Motorsport" is the most sought-after unofficial crown in the world of racing. It consists of winning the three most prestigious car races — the Indianapolis 500, the Monaco Grand Prix, and 24 Hours of Le Mans. Graham Hill is the only driver who has ever been able to pull it off.

CHAPTER 6

TRYING TO HELP

James Davison drove a race-ready Aston Martin in a 2015 United SportCar race.

Many people work together to make sure each sports car race is exciting, fast, and safe. One of the most important crews at a racetrack is the emergency and safety responders. These men and women are the first trained **personnel** on the track after an accident. It is their job to make sure drivers are treated for any injuries.

personnel—people employed by or working for an organization

At a United SportsCar race in 2015, rescue crews responded to a crash at a Michigan track. Near the end of the race Jan Helen slid his Porsche 911 into the barriers. The rescue truck was working on clearing the area. Just then a speeding Aston Martin driven by James Davison approached. In an accident no one saw coming, his car slammed into the back of the rescue truck. The truck's wheels left the ground. Rain had begun to fall, and the area was slick. Three other cars also wrecked near the scene of the damaged safety truck.

Everyone involved was examined by medical staff. The safety crew members were all taken to the hospital. Only one official had to remain there due to serious, but not life-threatening, injuries. The rest of the crew returned to the track.

CHAPTER 7

A PLACE ON TOP

In racing, it is always best to pull ahead of the pack, and not just because that means you're in the lead. It also helps drivers avoid collisions. When something goes wrong with one car, every driver behind it is at risk. And the closer cars are to each other, the greater the danger.

Every driver wants to avoid a pileup. That wasn't possible during a GT Tour race in 2015, in Navarra, Spain. As a pack of cars entered a tight bend, one Porsche race car started to slide out of line. Behind it, drivers scrambled to stay out of the way. Some slowed and some tried to zip quickly away from the others. But two drivers could not avoid each other. Joffrey De Narda lost control of his car. It spun around, facing the oncoming cars. Driving straight toward De Narda and boxed in on both sides, Jules Gounon suddenly realized he had nowhere to go but up. He drove up on top of De Narda's car! His wheels dangled on either side of De Narda's roof. The race continued without the two stuck cars, and a crane was called to remove the two-car pileup.

Crashes can be expensive. Both cars involved in this pileup were valued at $300,000 each.

CHAPTER 8

EXCITEMENT ON OPENING DAY

Opening day is always a great day at the racetrack. Sports car fans gather to enjoy the festivities. Drivers look forward to starting off their racing season. The 2016 British GT Championship opener in Kent, England, saw more than just the typical excitement.

Two drivers entered the race in Aston Martin sports cars. Phil Dryburgh and Matthew Graham were both aiming to take their cars to the finish line. The two men were entering a slight bend in the track when Graham bumped into Dryburgh's car. This lifted Dryburgh's two left wheels off the ground. Graham then slid under Dryburgh's car and launched it into the air. Graham spun off the track and across the grass. Behind him, Dryburgh's car flipped over repeatedly before coming to a stop. It landed on its wheels, but the damage done was too much to continue. Thankfully, both drivers walked away from the wreck.

A Manor Nissan leads during Round 2 of the 2016 FIA World Endurance Championship at Silverstone Circuit in Northamptonshire, England.

WILD!

The famous fictional spy James Bond drives an Aston Martin. The first movie to include an Aston Martin sports car was 1946's *Goldfinger*, and since then the car has appeared in every Bond film.

LOSING THE LEAD

During endurance races sports car drivers work in teams. This allows drivers to remain fresh and focused when they are behind the wheel. It also means that drivers must rely on their teammates to continue any lead or advantage they gain.

In 2016 Brendon Hartley joined the World Endurance Championship 6 Hours of Silverstone with his team. Mark Webber, his New Zealand teammate, drove just before him. He had a successful race, and when he turned over control of his Porsche to Hartley, the team was enjoying a 40-second lead. The team was in good spirits, as they entered the race as defending champions.

Brendon Hartley

A total of 33 cars entered the World Endurance Championship 6 Hours of Silverstone in 2016.

Hartley took over two hours into the race. As he approached a turn in the track, he tried to pass Michael Wainright on the outside. Hartley's car clipped the edge of Wainright's car, sending them both off the track. Hartley launched into the air and spun. His Porsche crashed to the ground, and both cars came to a rest in the safety gravel next to the track.

"I feel very upset for the team," Hartley said after the crash. He had not only lost the team's lead, but also taken them out of the race. It was a disappointing end to an important race, felt by every driver.

CHAPTER 10

WEATHER GETS IN THE WAY

The Nürburgring GP-Strecke track is nearly 13 miles (20.9 km) long with a total of 73 turns.

There are many factors at play in a sports car race. The drivers and cars are the most important elements. But sometimes outside influences can affect the outcome of a race. Bad weather is a big one. When the skies are blue and winds are low, race cars can speed around tracks with more ease. When skies get dark and extreme weather is in the forecast, racetracks get more dangerous.

The track for the 24 Hours of Nürburgring in Nürburgring, Germany, is one of the most challenging racecourses in the world. The forecast before the 2016 race called for rain, but race officials decided to continue with the race.

Less than an hour into the race the rain became a torrential downpour. Hail pelted the track and sports cars alike. The storm made it difficult for drivers to see where they were going.

Drivers had completed only a few laps of the race when they began to lose control on the slippery track. They skidded sideways, hitting cars and the barriers. A total of 25 cars were involved in accidents.

The race was delayed due to the dangerous conditions. It wasn't continued until late in the day, when the weather had passed.

GLOSSARY

aerodynamic (air-oh-dye-NA-mik)—built to move easily through the air

class (KLASS)— a group of things that are similar in many ways

competitor (kuhm-PE-tuh-tuhr)—a person who tries to win a race or contest

endurance (en-DUR-enss)—the ability to keep doing an activity for long periods of time

Grand Prix (GRAND PREE)—any of a series of auto racing or motorcycling contests forming part of a championship series, held in various locations

grand touring (GRAND TOOR-ing)—a type of sports car built for long-distance racing and based on models available for consumers

personnel (puhr-suh-NEL)—people employed by or working for an organization

prototype (PROH-tuh-tipe)—a type of sports car, which is based on a model available to consumers, used at the highest level of racing

READ MORE

Bach, Rachel. *The Car Race*. Let's Race. Mankato, Minn.: Amicus Ink, 2017.

McCollum, Sean. *The World's Fastest Cars*. World Record Breakers. North Mankato, Minn.: Capstone Press, 2017.

Worms, Penny. *Sports Cars*. Motormania. Mankato, Minn.: Smart Apple Media, 2016.

INTERNET SITES

FactHound offers a safe, fun way to find Internet sites related to this book. All of the sites on FactHound have been researched by our staff.

Here's all you do:

Visit *www.facthound.com*

Type in this code: 9781515774051

Check out projects, games and lots more at
www.capstonekids.com

INDEX